REPTILES

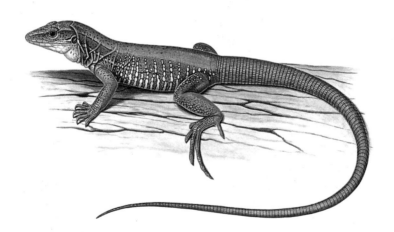

REPTILES

Consultant Editor
Dr Mark Hutchinson

FOG CITY PRESS

Published by Fog City Press
814 Montgomery Street
San Francisco, CA 94133 USA

Copyright © 2005 Weldon Owen Pty Ltd
This edition printed 2007

Chief Executive Officer, Weldon Owen Group: John Owen
Chief Executive Officer and President: Terry Newell
Chief Financial Officer, Weldon Owen Inc.: Simon Fraser
Vice President International Sales: Stuart Laurence
Publisher: Sheena Coupe
Creative Director: Sue Burk
Managing Editor (revised edition): Karen Penzes
Project Management: Limelight Press Pty Ltd
Project Editor: John Mapps
Series Design: Nika Markovtzev
Project Designer: Jacqueline Richards
Editorial Coordinators: Helen Flint, Lucie Parker
Production Director: Chris Hemesath
Sales Manager: Emily Bartle
Cover Design: Kelly Booth

ISBN-10: 1-74089-560-6
ISBN-13: 978-1-74089-560-6

Color reproduction by SC (Sang Choy) International Pte Ltd
Printed by SNP Leefung Printers Ltd
Printed in China

A Weldon Owen Production

Contents

ORIGINS OF
REPTILES

The First Reptiles

About 50 million years after the first amphibians appeared, the first reptiles evolved from an amphibian ancestor. The earliest reptiles looked like small lizards. A hundred million years later, reptiles had replaced amphibians as the dominant land animals. Early reptiles developed into the first dinosaurs, which dominated the land, and into a range of other reptiles that flew in the skies and swam in the seas.

EARLY REPTILE
The earliest known reptile is
Hylonomus, which was about
8 inches (20 cm) long.

DID YOU KNOW?
**The earliest reptiles
probably hunted and
fed on insects.**

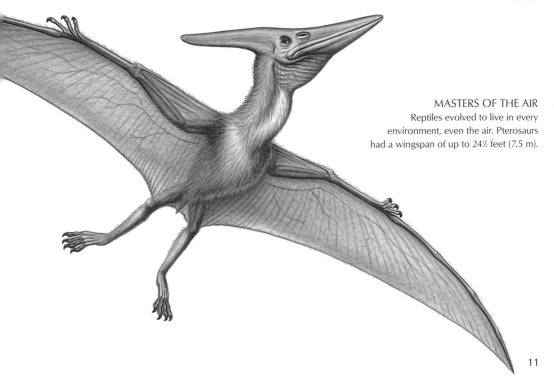

MASTERS OF THE AIR
Reptiles evolved to live in every
environment, even the air. Pterosaurs
had a wingspan of up to 24½ feet (7.5 m).

11

The Age of Reptiles

From 250 to 65 million years ago, reptiles dominated the land, sea, and sky. As well as dinosaurs, there were ocean-going plesiosaurs, flying pterosaurs, lizards, snakes, crocodiles, turtles, and tuataras. All large reptiles, except crocodiles and turtles, became extinct about 65 million years ago, but the ancestors of today's reptiles survived to evolve into thousands of different species.

REPTILES RULE
Prehistoric reptiles ranged from small turtles and flying lizards to gigantic dinosaurs such as the *Stegosaurus* (far right) and creatures with a "sail" on their back.

Dinosaur Diversity

The first dinosaurs appeared 228 million years ago. A huge number of dinosaur types developed from them—we know of at least 1,000 different ones. Some were the size of chickens. Others were the biggest meat-eaters the world has known, such as the 46 foot (14 m) *Tyrannosaurus*. Still others were plant-eating giants: *Saltasaurus* reached 39 feet (12 m) in length, and *Triceratops* was about 30 feet (9 m) long.

CRETACEOUS PARADE
Dinosaurs were at their most varied and numerous during the Cretaceous period, between 165 and 145 million years ago.

SMALL BEGINNINGS

Like the reptiles of today, dinosaurs laid eggs.

Triceratops

Corythosaurus

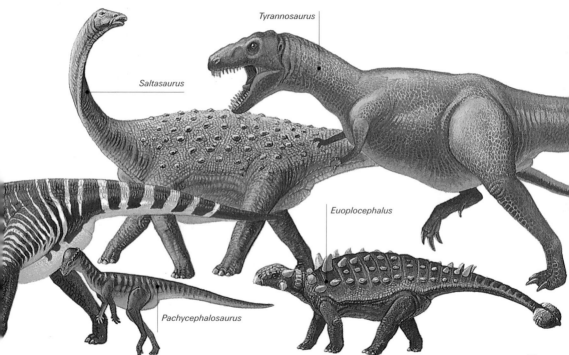

Saltasaurus

Tyrannosaurus

Euoplocephalus

Pachycephalosaurus

Ancient Marine Reptiles

While dinosaurs ruled the land, their cousin reptiles dominated the sea. The oceans were home to plesiosaurs, pliosaurs, ichthyosaurs, marine turtles, crocodiles, and other reptiles. Plesiosaurs had long necks and ate small creatures. Pliosaurs had large heads and short necks, and tackled larger prey with their strong teeth and claws. Ichthyosaurs had streamlined bodies and sharklike fins and a tail.

The pliosaur *Peloneustes* was 10 feet (3 m) long.

Nothosaurus was 10 feet (3 m) long.

MARINE MASTERS
The oceans were full of marine reptiles of many different shapes and sizes. They competed to feed on fish, small sea creatures, and each other.

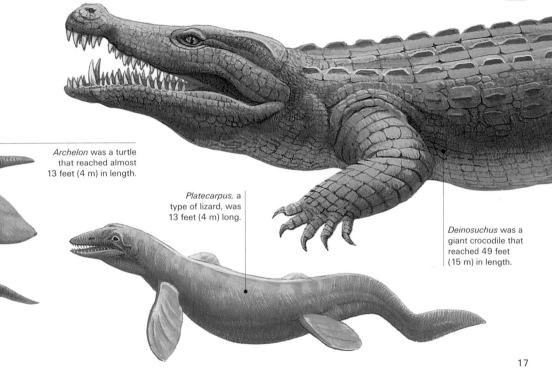

Archelon was a turtle that reached almost 13 feet (4 m) in length.

Platecarpus, a type of lizard, was 13 feet (4 m) long.

Deinosuchus was a giant crocodile that reached 49 feet (15 m) in length.

ALL ABOUT
REPTILES

Turtles and Tortoises

Turtles and tortoises are known as chelonians. They are the only reptiles that have a shell built into the skeleton. Like other reptiles, they lay eggs. Most turtles live in water, but tortoises are land dwellers. Sea turtles live in the oceans. Freshwater turtles occur in ponds, lakes, streams, and rivers. All sea turtles and some freshwater turtles leave the water only to lay eggs. Other species move between water and land. Land tortoises live in dry areas where there are no open bodies of water.

A REAL STINKER

The southern loggerhead musk turtle lives in fresh water in southern North America. When disturbed, these turtles release a very strong smell.

DID YOU KNOW?

The smallest chelonian is the speckled padloper. It is only 3¼ inches (95 mm) long.

BRIGHT BOY

This male painted turtle has a brightly colored shell, head, and legs. It lives in ponds and rivers in North America and has a 10 inch (25 cm) long shell.

BEAUTIFULLY MARKED

The shell of the radiated tortoise has beautiful markings. This land tortoise is found in dry regions of southwest Madagascar, where it is endangered.

Chelonians Up Close

The shells of chelonians set them apart from all other reptiles. The shell consists of two parts: the upper part is called the carapace, and the lower part is the plastron. Each part has an inner bony layer and an outer layer of horny plates (scutes). Chelonians are divided into two groups according to the way they draw their head into their shell. One group has a flexible neck that can be pulled back straight into the shell. The members of the other group bend their neck sideways and curl their head under the front of their upper shell. Either method protects the chelonian from enemies.

Scutes (outer layer)

Hindfoot

DID YOU KNOW?

Scutes are made of keratin, the same substance as the outer layer of a fingernail.

INSIDE THE SHELL
The shell is attached to the spine and ribs. Scutes make up the shell's outer layer; a bony layer lies underneath. The flexible neck bones allow the animal to draw its head into its shell.

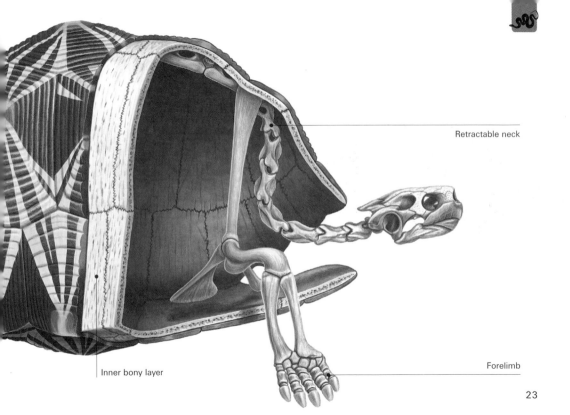

Retractable neck

Inner bony layer

Forelimb

Shell Shapes

SEMI-TERRESTRIAL TURTLE
Semi-terrestrial (semi-land) turtles divide their time between the land and the water. Their shells are not as high as those of land tortoises, but not as flat as those of sea turtles.

SEA TURTLE
Sea turtles are fast swimmers in the oceans, and come ashore only to lay eggs. They have light shells that are streamlined to make swimming easier.

LAND TORTOISE
Land tortoises have thick, dome-shaped shells for protection from predators. As their shells are very strong and heavy, land tortoises move slowly.

POND TURTLE
Pond turtles spend most of their time in small bodies of fresh water. They have small, flattened, usually lighter shells, to make swimming easier.

Suitable Limbs

The legs of turtles and tortoises have evolved to suit the different environments in which they live. Land tortoises have column-shaped legs with large claws to grip the earth. Pond turtles need to move on land and in the water, so they have webbing between their claws. Sea turtles have large front flippers to push them quickly through the water.

FAST SWIMMERS
Sea turtles are built for life in the oceans. As well as large front flippers, they have light, streamlined shells. On land, however, they are clumsy and have to drag themselves along.

LAND TORTOISE
Column-shaped legs; large claws

POND TURTLE
Webbing between the claws

SEA TURTLE
Legs have evolved into flippers.

Turtle Love

Mating behavior varies from the male simply mounting the female, to elaborate courtship rituals. Courtship in tortoises usually involves some head-bobbing, with the male head-butting and biting the female.

MATING TIME
Sea turtles mate for the first time when they are several years old, then return to the same beach to breed.

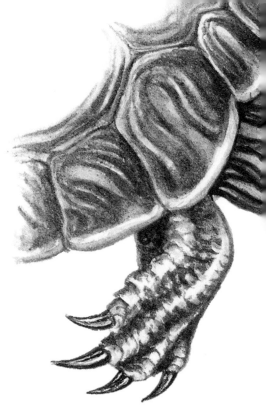

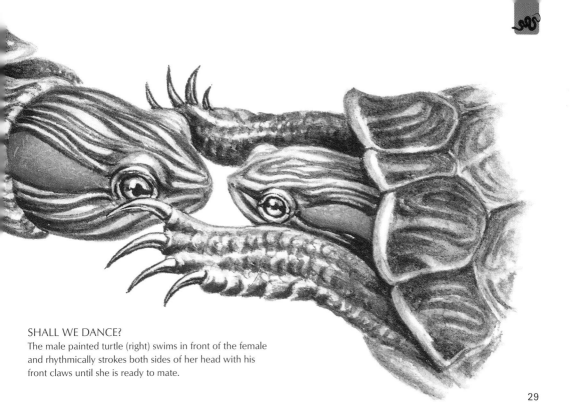

SHALL WE DANCE?

The male painted turtle (right) swims in front of the female and rhythmically strokes both sides of her head with his front claws until she is ready to mate.

Fending for Themselves

After mating, turtles and tortoises lay their eggs in shallow burrows, usually near the areas where they live and feed. Females lay the eggs and cover the nest. The eggs of most species hatch after a few months. In many species, the hatchlings spend the winter in the egg chamber and come outside during the spring. After the eggs are laid, the parents show no further interest in the young. From the day they leave the nest, the hatchlings must fend for themselves.

LAYING EGGS
Land tortoises lay their eggs in nests scraped out of the soil, burying them afterward. Burying the eggs keeps them at a constant temperature.

INDEPENDENCE DAY
Chelonians are independent from the moment they leave the egg.

DID YOU KNOW?

Only about 1 in 100 turtle hatchlings survives to become an adult.

ON ITS OWN

A newly hatched sea turtle makes its way to the ocean. With no protection from their parents, many hatchlings are killed by predators such as birds.

Feeding Time

Sea turtles eat shellfish, fish, jellyfish, and sea grasses. Semi-terrestrial turtles hunt on land and water, and eat both plant and animal food. Young land tortoises eat worms and insects as well as plants. Adult land tortoises, which move too slowly to catch animals, eat flowers, fruits, and plants.

SHARP JAWS
Turtles and tortoises, such as this giant land tortoise, do not have teeth. They use their sharp-edged jaws to grasp and cut plant and animal food.

BERRY TREAT
This eastern box turtle is just about to devour some wild strawberries. As well as plants, it eats snails, slugs, insects, and earthworms.

WORMS FOR VARIETY
A wood turtle makes a meal of an earthworm. These turtles venture short distances from their watery homes to find food, which includes both plants and animals.

In and Out of Water

Most turtles and tortoises live in or near fresh water such as lakes, rivers, and swamps. Almost all freshwater turtles have webbed feet with claws, and light, flat shells. To feed, they lie underwater, waiting for their prey of insects and fish to come past. Hunting on land and in the water, semi-terrestrial turtles eat various plants and small animals. In winter, some of them hibernate in mud under water or in burrows on land.

GONE FISHING
An American snapping turtle snaps up a fish. This species spends most of its time in water.

INTO THE TREES
The big-headed turtle of Vietnam is a poor swimmer. It is a good climber, however, and can sometimes be seen soaking up the sun on the branches of trees and bushes.

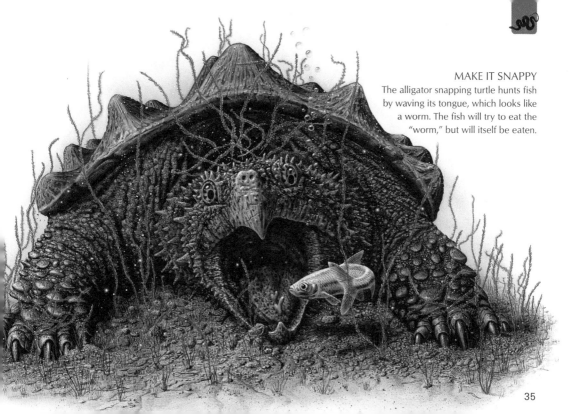

MAKE IT SNAPPY
The alligator snapping turtle hunts fish by waving its tongue, which looks like a worm. The fish will try to eat the "worm," but will itself be eaten.

Land Tortoises—Little and Large

There are about 40 species of land tortoises. Many of them live in dry environments or deserts. Most have high-domed shells to protect them from predators. As their shells are strong and heavy, land tortoises move slowly. Most species are plant-eaters, though some also eat insects.

HEAVYWEIGHT
Galápagos tortoises weigh between 330 and 440 pounds (150–200 kg).

SIZE RANGE
At just over 3 inches (8 cm) long, the speckled padloper is the world's smallest land tortoise. Other land tortoises shown here range in size from the 4 inch (10 cm) long Madagascan spider tortoises to the 8 inch (20 cm) long South American tortoises and the wheelbarrow-sized giants of the Aldabra and Galápagos islands.

Keeping Cool

Many land tortoises live in hot, dry areas of the world, such as deserts. In these places, tortoises have to be careful not to overheat or dry out. They are active only during the coolest times of the day—the morning and the late afternoon or evening. During the hottest part of the day, they lie in the shade of shrubs and trees or in burrows in the soil.

TUCKED IN

As well as keeping cool, turtles and tortoises must keep moist. The ornate box turtle draws its head and legs into its domed shell to protect itself from drying out and from predators.

COOL HOME

The gopher tortoise of North America lives in deserts. Active in the early morning and evening, it digs a burrow and retreats into it during the hottest part of the day. The burrow can also be used to keep warm in winter.

Galápagos Giants

Giant tortoises live on the Galápagos Islands in the Pacific Ocean. Those on the large, wetter islands have developed big dome-like shells. Tortoises on the smaller, drier islands where plants grow tall have long legs and a smaller shell called a saddleback. This shell is raised in front so that the tortoises can stretch their neck and reach up to the plants.

SADDLEBACK STRETCH
In dry times, giant saddleback tortoises get water and food from tall cactus plants. When it rains, dozens of tortoises collect around puddles and drink as much as they can.

NO NEED FOR LUNCH
If necessary, Galápagos tortoises can go without food for up to a year.

Sea Turtles

Sea turtles are found in all the tropical and subtropical oceans of the world. They eat fish, jellyfish, sponges, crabs, clams, mussels, sea urchins, and marine plants such as seaweed. They use their large front limbs like paddles to move through the water. The smaller rear limbs act as rudders. Sea turtles use the ocean currents to help them search for food.

BURST OF SPEED
Sea turtles usually swim slowly, helped by currents. But they can put on a quick burst to escape from predators such as sharks, reaching speeds of up to 18 miles (29 km) per hour.

Life at Sea

Sea turtles spend almost all their life at sea. The males never leave the water and the females do so only to lay eggs. The two sexes travel vast distances across the oceans to breed. They meet at sea near the beach where the nest will be. After mating, the female comes ashore at night to lay the eggs. She lays as many as 200 of them. Many sea turtles are endangered because of hunting by humans.

DID YOU KNOW?

Sea turtles often sunbathe at the ocean surface on floating fields of seaweed.

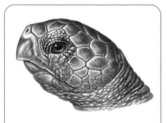

EYE WASH
Sea turtles produce "tears" from special glands close to the eyes to get rid of salt.

LONG DISTANCE
Some green turtles swim from the coast of Brazil to beaches in the mid-Atlantic to lay their eggs.

RACE FOR SURVIVAL
Newly born flatback turtles dig themselves out of the sand and race to the sea. They stick together as a group to try to escape being eaten by predators.

Softshell Turtles

Instead of a hard shell, these turtles have a leathery skin, which is light and flexible. They hide on the muddy beds of freshwater rivers, lakes, and streams, and eat mollusks, insects, crustaceans, worms, frogs, and fish.

AT HOME UNDER WATER

Softshell turtles are adapted for life in the water. As well as a light shell, they have webbed feet and snorkel-shaped snouts for breathing beneath the surface.

SPINY SHELL EDGE
The eastern spiny softshell turtle is a colorful species of southeastern North America.

TURTLE PANCAKE
With its head and legs retracted, the smooth softshell turtle looks a bit like a pancake.

Crocodilians

Crocodiles, alligators, caimans, and gharials are known as crocodilians. Most species live in tropical parts of the world, in Asia, Africa, Australia, and the Americas. They are excellent swimmers and can also walk on land. All are stealthy predators. Among the crocodilians are some of the largest and most dangerous reptiles in the world.

Crocodilian Characteristics

Crocodilians have long, narrow bodies covered in a leathery skin. They spend much of their time in the water, where they swim using powerful bladelike tails. Crocodilians have short legs and cannot walk far on land. They have extra eyelids that are transparent, and close to keep the water out. Their large mouths have many sharp teeth for killing and tearing apart prey.

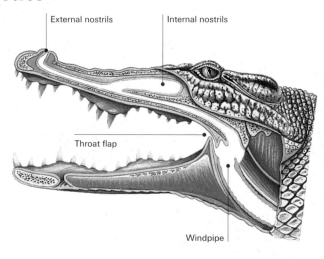

External nostrils | Internal nostrils

Throat flap

Windpipe

UNDERWATER ADAPTATIONS
A crocodilian can breathe while half under water because it has external nostrils that remain above the water. It also has a throat flap to stop water going down the windpipe when the animal is killing prey under water.

SALTWATER CROCODILE

The largest species of crocodilian is the saltwater crocodile. It can grow to 23 feet (7 m) in length.

TOMISTOMA

The tomistoma or false gharial is a medium-sized crocodilian. It reaches a length of about 13 feet (4 m).

CUVIER'S DWARF CAIMAN

This is the smallest crocodilian. It is 5 feet (1.5 m) long fully grown.

A Head and Side View

Crocodilian snouts vary in shape and size, according to their diets and the way they live. Gharials live in fast-flowing rivers and feed on fish, so their snout is narrow and full of small teeth, good for gripping fish. Alligators, caimans, and crocodiles feed on larger animals and have a big head with powerful jaws and large teeth. Alligators and caimans live in swamps with lots of vegetation. With their stronger heads and variable sized teeth, the broader-headed crocodilians can trap and hold a wide variety of prey.

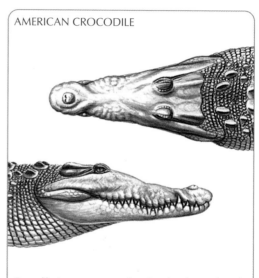

AMERICAN CROCODILE

Crocodiles' snouts are usually pointed and not as broad as those of alligators. When crocodiles close their mouth, the fourth tooth in the lower jaw is just visible.

DID YOU KNOW?

Nile crocodiles have been seen to kill fully grown Cape buffaloes.

BLACK CAIMAN

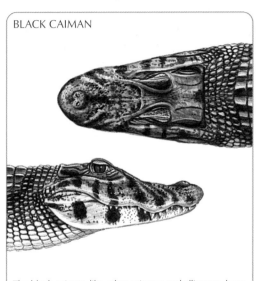

The black caiman, like other caimans and alligators, has a broad, heavy snout. When alligators and caimans close their mouth, no lower teeth can be seen.

GHARIAL

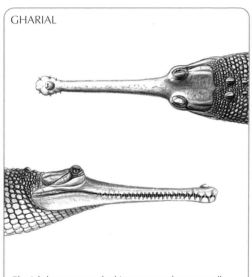

Gharials have extremely thin snouts and many small, pointed teeth. The teeth are excellent for holding on to the slippery bodies of its main prey, fish.

Sneaky Predators

Crocodilians are sneaky hunters. They float easily and lie just under the water with only their eyes, ears, and nostrils showing. They drift slowly toward their prey and attack with a sudden rush. Crocodilians' teeth are designed to grip, not cut. Because they cannot chew their food, they swallow prey in one gulp or tear it into large pieces.

Mother Care

Female crocodilians look after their eggs and young more carefully than most other reptiles. They lay eggs in nests or bury them in holes in the sand or soil. Many predators, including fish, lizards, mammals, birds, and sometimes even other crocodilians, would like to eat newly hatched crocodilians. The mother guards her hatchlings for several weeks or more until the young can fend for themselves.

CARRIED IN COMFORT
This hatchling alligator is being carried in its mother's mouth.

Guarding the Nest

Female crocodilians guard their nests, scaring away predators such as large lizards, mammals, and birds. The eggs take 60 to 100 days to develop, depending on the species and the temperature of the nest. The nest's temperature determines the sex of the hatchlings. The highest and lowest temperatures usually produce females, while in-between temperatures usually produce males.

PREDATOR-FREE
Young crocodiles in a crocodile farm are protected from predators.

MOTHER IS WATCHING
A female crocodile guards her nest, which is covered with warm, rotting plant material, for up to 100 days. She does not leave the nest and will attack any intruder that comes too close.

59

Crocodiles

There are 13 species of crocodiles. They range from medium to large, and have quite narrow snouts. Crocodiles and alligators look very similar, but you can tell them apart by looking at their teeth. The fourth tooth in a crocodile's lower jaw is still visible when the crocodile closes its mouth. All of the alligator's upper teeth fit into pits in the upper jaw and cannot be seen. Crocodiles live in a variety of freshwater and saltwater habitats, such as lagoons, swamps, beaches, and rivers, in Australia, Africa, North and South America, and Asia.

WAITING FOR PREY
A crocodile lies partly submerged, waiting for its prey. When they strike, crocodiles move quickly through the water, lunge up onto the bank and pull the prey into the water. They then drown and eat the prey.

The Crocodile Walk

Crocodiles are good swimmers and spend most of their time in water, but sometimes they must move over land. When they need to move rapidly, usually to retreat to water, they use an awkward, sprawling action. On slippery or muddy surfaces, they slide or crawl on their belly. Over long distances on dry land, a crocodile walks in a similar way to mammals. Some species can gallop quickly to escape danger.

DID YOU KNOW?

When a crocodile gallops, all four limbs may be in the air at the same time.

Walking involves keeping the belly well off the ground.

ON THE MOVE
Crocodiles often crawl the short distance from a muddy riverbank to the water. On dry land, they lift up their body and walk, dragging their tail. Crocodiles that can gallop, only do so for short distances.

A crocodile crawls on its belly just before entering the water.

A galloping crocodile moves like a horse at high speed.

OUT FOR A WALK
A Nile crocodile walks slowly across a mudflat toward its real home, the river.

Gharials

Gharials have long, narrow snouts. They feed mainly on fish, but also eat insects, frogs, snakes, and birds. There are two species. The gharial lives in fast-flowing rivers and hill streams in India, Pakistan, Bangladesh, Nepal, Bhutan, and Burma. It reaches 20 feet (6 m) in length. The tomistoma, or false gharial, inhabits freshwater lakes, swamps, and rivers in parts of Thailand, Malaysia, and Indonesia. It grows to 13 feet (4 m).

UNDER THREAT
Habitat destruction and hunting have endangered the tomistoma.

FISH-EATER
The gharial's extremely thin snout and its many small, pointed teeth are ideal for grasping the struggling, slippery bodies of fish.

Table Manners

Unlike other reptiles, crocodilians do not chew their food.
Instead, they swallow prey whole or tear it into large pieces
before swallowing. Most species swallow stones and hard
objects, called gastroliths, which help to break down the
food so it can be digested.

MESSY EATER
Crocodiles tear up their prey into
big chunks before swallowing it.

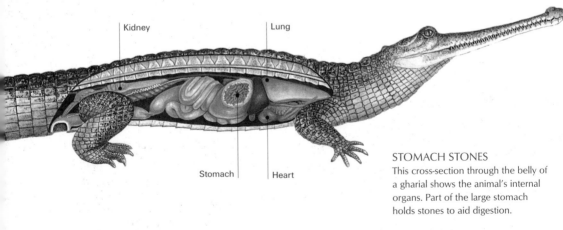

Kidney

Lung

Stomach

Heart

STOMACH STONES
This cross-section through the belly of
a gharial shows the animal's internal
organs. Part of the large stomach
holds stones to aid digestion.

Alligators and Caimans

Alligators and their close relatives, caimans, have a broader snout than crocodiles, and grow to be almost as big. There are two species of alligators, the American alligator, which can grow to 19 feet (6 m), and the much smaller and rarer Chinese alligator. The several species of caimans live in various parts of Central and South America. The largest is the black caiman, which can reach about 16 feet (5 m) in length.

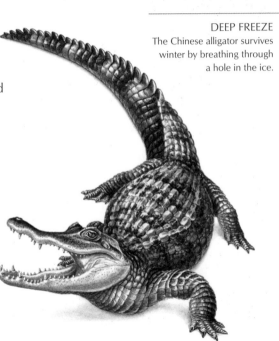

DEEP FREEZE
The Chinese alligator survives winter by breathing through a hole in the ice.

COMMON CAIMAN
The common caiman of South America grows to about 8 feet (2.5 m) in length and looks like a small crocodile. It eats insects, crabs, snails, and fish.

Jump Shot

Crocodiles and alligators rely heavily on their ability to surprise their prey by suddenly exploding into action. Most of the time, the kill takes place in or under water. But sometimes it happens in midair. If a bird comes too close to the water, a crocodile or alligator makes a jump shot, lunging upward and lifting its body almost clear of the water. Its massive jaws do the rest.

UNDERWATER HUNTER
A Johnston's crocodile puts on a
burst of speed to catch fish.

LUNGE FOR LUNCH
American alligators often hunt near waterbird colonies where the birds eat the fish that gather there. Occasionally an alligator will leap from the water to catch a bird such as this egret chick, which has fallen from its nest.

DID YOU KNOW?

Two species of crocodiles attack humans: the Nile and the saltwater crocodile.

Lizards at Large

No other group of reptiles has developed into as many different forms as the lizards. They range from tiny legless wormlike creatures to giant monitors with powerful limbs.

LIZARDS OF THE SEA
Marine iguanas of the Galápagos Islands live in
large colonies throughout most of the year.

Looking at Lizards

There are about 3,750 species of lizards in the world. They come in all shapes and sizes, from a tiny gecko to the 10 foot (3 m) long Komodo dragon. Some are short and fat; others are legless and look like snakes. Some lizards are brightly colored, while others are dull and blend into the background. Most are predators, and eat everything from ants and insects to other lizards and animals as large as goats.

TINY LIZARD
Most lizards are small, which allows them to occupy numerous habitats. This tiny anole is clinging to a stem of grass.

LITTLE LEOPARD
The 8 inch (20 cm) leopard gecko gets its name from its beautifully patterned skin.

VENOMOUS MONSTER
The gila monster lives in arid regions of Mexico and the United States. It is one of only two lizards to have a venomous bite.

Lizard Bodies

Boyd's forest dragon puffs out its throat flap and shows off its scaly crests to communicate with other forest dragons.

The Argus goanna uses its tail as a prop to stand up and look around.

LOW PROFILE

A flat body helps this desert short-horned lizard hide from predators.

SNAKELIKE SHAPE

The legless lizard looks very similar to a snake. It has a streamlined body that makes it easy to move in and out of narrow places.

ATHLETIC HUNTER

A slim, athletic body makes this perentie an excellent long-distance runner.

STANDARD MODEL

A wall lizard has the most common lizard body shape.

Every Tail Tells a Story

Some lizards have tails that look like leaves; others have tails that look like heads. Both types of tails fool predators. Some tails are used to hold on to branches or to store fat. Skinks can shed their tail. If a predator grabs a skink's tail, the tail breaks off and stays in the predator's mouth while the skink escapes.

FAT TAIL
Shingleback tails store fat—a source of water and energy.

FLAT TAIL
Leaf-tailed geckos' tails are flattened and camouflaged.

DID YOU KNOW?

Many monitors use their tail as a club to beat up attackers or prey.

TAIL AS ANCHOR
When a predator comes near, the spiny-tailed monitor uses the spines on its tail to wedge itself into a rock crevice, making it hard to drag out.

STREAMLINED TAIL
Most skinks' tails are long and streamlined.

GRIPPING TAIL
Tree-living chameleons use their tail to grip twigs.

Lizard Legs

Most lizards have four well-developed legs. Some, such as the Australian frilled-neck lizard, can run on their two large back legs for short distances. Other lizards have small limbs, or no limbs at all. These lizards usually burrow in the ground, or live in places where limbs would be of little use, such as dense grass or under leaf litter.

Close-up of hairlike structures on a gecko's toe.

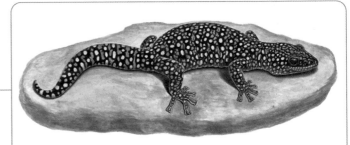

Geckos like this one climb well because their toe pads have hairlike structures (left) that cling to rough surfaces.

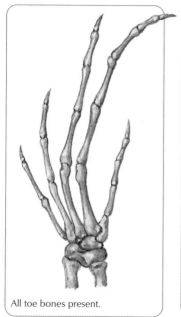

All toe bones present.

Two sets of toe bones lost.

DISAPPEARING LEGS

Some lizards have small limbs, or sometimes none at all. This has helped them survive because they move like little snakes, wriggling through soft sand or dense bush. Lizards that spend the most time in the thickest surroundings have the smallest limbs. The bones become smaller, and in some cases, one of more sets of toe bones do not develop at all.

No toes

Tongues

Most lizards use their tongues to help them eat, but they also use them to track down prey or to find a mate. They do this by "tasting" the air and ground.

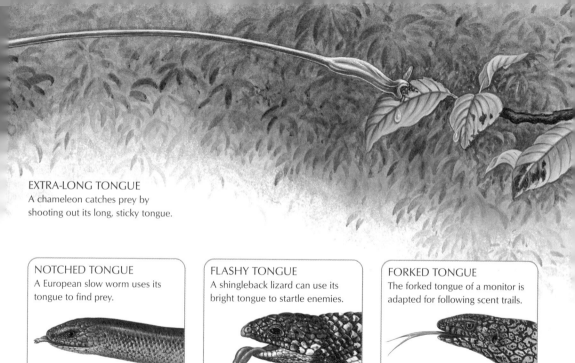

EXTRA-LONG TONGUE
A chameleon catches prey by shooting out its long, sticky tongue.

NOTCHED TONGUE
A European slow worm uses its tongue to find prey.

FLASHY TONGUE
A shingleback lizard can use its bright tongue to startle enemies.

FORKED TONGUE
The forked tongue of a monitor is adapted for following scent trails.

83

Watching the World

Lizards that live above the ground need good eyesight and large eyes. Those that spend their life beneath the ground have tiny eyes because they rely on senses other than sight. Lizards that are active at night need to be able to see in the dark. They have big eyes and their pupils—the transparent "holes" that let light into the eyes—are large, vertical slits. At night, these open wide to let in as much light as possible.

BEADY EYES
The bulging eyes of a chameleon move independently. This means that this lizard can see backward and forward at the same time without moving.

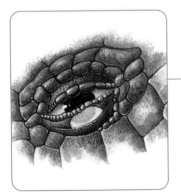

WINDOW WITH A VIEW
Many lizards, such as skinks (left), have a small clear area on their lower eyelids (far left). This allows them to watch for predators with closed eyes.

DID YOU KNOW?
Most geckos do not have eyelids and use their tongue to clean their eyes.

Temperature Control

Like other reptiles, lizards control their body temperature with their behavior. To warm up, they move into the sun or onto a warm surface and expose as much of the body as they can to the heat. To cool down, they expose as little of the body as possible to the heat, or they move into the shade of a crevice. Many desert and tropical lizards are active at night because the night-time temperatures in these places are mild.

COOLING DOWN
In hot weather, a collared lizard cools down by opening its mouth to allow its saliva to evaporate.

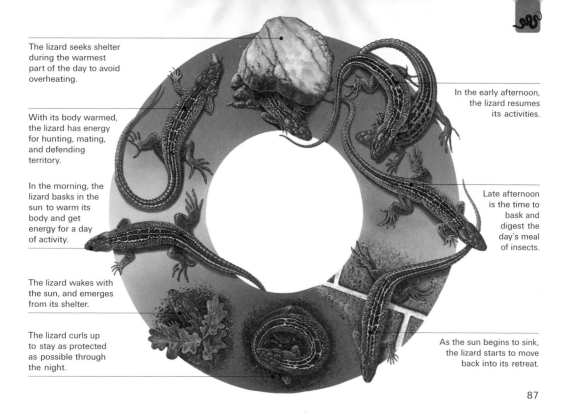

The lizard seeks shelter during the warmest part of the day to avoid overheating.

With its body warmed, the lizard has energy for hunting, mating, and defending territory.

In the morning, the lizard basks in the sun to warm its body and get energy for a day of activity.

The lizard wakes with the sun, and emerges from its shelter.

The lizard curls up to stay as protected as possible through the night.

In the early afternoon, the lizard resumes its activities.

Late afternoon is the time to bask and digest the day's meal of insects.

As the sun begins to sink, the lizard starts to move back into its retreat.

Day and Night

Most lizards do all their activities, such as feeding and mating, during the day. Lizards that are active in the daytime must be careful not to overheat. Some lizards, such as geckos, are active at night. They emerge shortly after dark (when it is still warm) to hunt for prey at a time when other lizards are not around.

ALL-DAY IGUANA
Most desert lizards avoid the hottest part of the day. But the desert iguana goes about its business during the whole day, even when temperatures are very high.

NIGHT HUNTER
Most geckos, such as this banded gecko, are active either at night or in the near-dark hours of twilight and before sunset. They hunt for insects and spiders.

SHADES OF THE DAY
In the cool parts of the day, the skin of the rhinoceros iguana is dark to absorb the heat of the Sun. The skin is a lighter color during the hottest parts of the day to reflect heat.

Living in Dry Places

Lizards that live in dry places have to cope with high temperatures and a lack of water. Some species are active at night to escape the heat of the day. Daytime species burrow into cool sand or hide in crevices and beneath rocks during the hottest part of the day. Most desert lizards get most of the water they need from their food. All desert lizards produce droppings that are almost dry, to minimize water loss.

WATER COLLECTOR
The Australian thorny devil lives in deserts. The edges of the small scales on their legs and body form tiny channels that act like a sponge and carry water over its skin to its mouth.

DID YOU KNOW?
"Sand swimmers" are desert lizards that seem to be able to swim through loose sand.

FRINGE-TOED LIZARD
The feathery scales on this desert-living lizard's feet help to grip sand.

DESERT GECKO
One gecko from Africa's Namib Desert uses webbed feet to move across fine sand.

Mating Signals

Male and female marine iguanas of the Galápagos Islands are usually a grayish-black color. In the mating season, the spiny crests and front limbs of the males turn green and the sides of their body become a rusty red. These changes let the females know that the males are ready to mate.

Reproduction

Most lizards lay eggs. Some geckos
and skinks lay only one, while larger
lizards may lay forty. Other lizards,
such as the Australian blue-tongue skink, give birth to
fully formed young. Eggs are protected inside the female's
body, and the developing young are nourished by yolk, in the
same way as young that grow in eggs outside the body.

The Next Generation

A few lizards guard their eggs against predators, but most simply lay their eggs, cover them with soil and leaves, and leave them. Lizards are able to look after themselves as soon as they hatch, but there are many predators, such as birds and spiders, that try to eat the hatchlings.

SINGLE PARENTS
Some lizards, such as this whiptail lizard, are all females. There are no males, and eggs develop and hatch (daughters only!) without fertilization.

HOUSE GUESTS
Some species of monitors keep their eggs warm and safe by burying them in termite mounds. The female has to scrape away the hard soil to help her hatchlings escape.

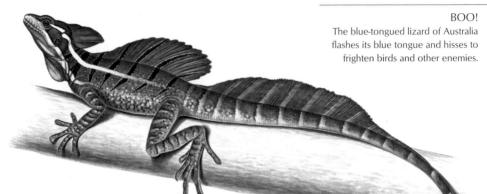

BOO!
The blue-tongued lizard of Australia flashes its blue tongue and hisses to frighten birds and other enemies.

Defense and Escape

Lizards have many enemies. Spiders, scorpions, other lizards, snakes, birds, and mammals all prey on them. Some lizards have special tactics to defend themselves or to escape from an attacker. Most lizards are well camouflaged and keep still until a predator passes by. Chameleons can change their color to blend in with the background. Some lizards poke out their colored tongue to startle attackers.

RUNNING ON WATER
The South American basilisk has a unique way of getting away from predators. Fringes on its toes allow it to run for short distances on its long hind legs across the surface of water.

Body Language

Most lizards live alone. They come into contact with other members of their species only for courtship and mating, and to fight over living areas. Lizards communicate using body language. They can raise their crest, extend or curl their dewlap (flap of skin on the throat), wave a front limb, thrash their tail, or change color. All of these signs mean something, from "Keep away" to "I'm ready to mate."

PUSHING UP

Collared lizards communicate with each other by bobbing their heads up and down. If another lizard enters their territory, they threaten the invader by doing "push-ups" that make them look bigger.

CALM GREEN
Male chameleons normally have dull-colored skin that blends in with the background. In the case of this species, the main color is green.

THREATENING RED
If the male wants to warn another male chameleon away from its territory, it changes its skin tone to a much brighter color, such as red.

Escaping Danger

Running fast, out of a predator's reach, is a good way to escape. Some lizards extend their neck or throat crest, hiss, or swallow air to make themselves look bigger than an attacker (or too big to swallow). Many lizards have an unusual method of escape. If grabbed by the tail, they leave it behind. The wriggling tail distracts the predator.

BLOODY ENCOUNTER

The regal horned lizard squirts a stream of its own blood up to 3 feet (1 m) to frighten an attacker.

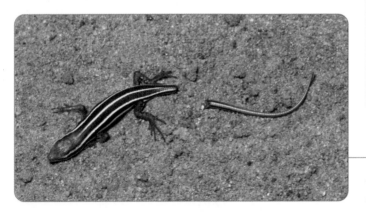

NEW TAIL
This lizard will soon grow a new tail after dropping it to distract a predator.

TOO BIG A MOUTHFUL
Bearded dragon lizards open their yellow mouths to surprise attackers. They also expand their throats to make themselves look too big for a predator to eat.

Self-Defense

Some lizards have sharp spines that can injure a predator's mouth, or slippery scales that make them hard to grip. The armadillo girdle-tailed lizard rolls itself into a spiky ball. The Gila monster and the Mexican beaded lizard can give attackers a poisonous bite. Monitors arch their long tail when threatened and will often use it as a weapon.

SPINES FOR DEFENSE
The desert horned lizard has a row of sharp spines along its tail and sides.

SCALES AND SPIKES

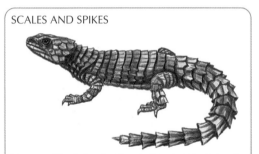

The armadillo girdle-tailed lizard of South Africa is heavily armored, with thick scales and spikes on its head and tail.

COVER-UP

When threatened, the lizard clamps its tail in its mouth and curls itself into a ball, protecting its soft belly.

Worm Lizards

Worm lizards spend most of their time underground. They burrow through soil with their hard, strong heads. Apart from one Mexican group that has small front legs, all others have no legs at all, and look like worms or snakes.

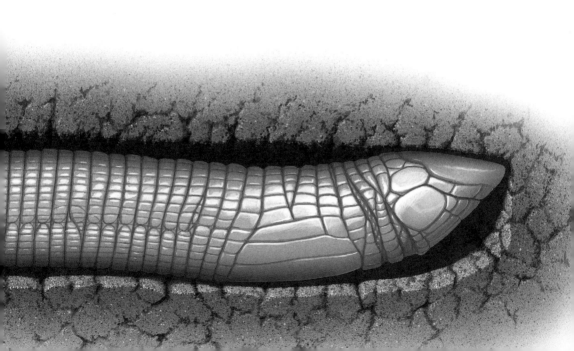

Different Heads

Worm lizards have cylinder-shaped bodies and create tunnels by burrowing with their heads. Different groups of worm lizards have different-shaped heads, depending on the method they use to burrow. Worm lizards have simple and sometimes invisible eyes. They have no openings for ears, but they can sense prey and predators through vibrations in the soil. They eat insects and other invertebrates.

DOWN BELOW
A section of the ground has been cut away to show a worm lizard lying inside its tunnel. These lizards spend most of their life underground.

DID YOU KNOW?

The Mexican worm lizard has paddle-like front legs it uses for digging.

SIDE-TO-SIDE DIGGER

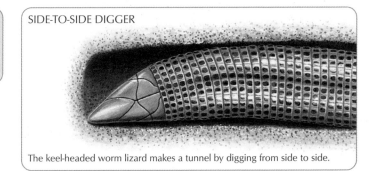

The keel-headed worm lizard makes a tunnel by digging from side to side.

CHISEL-HEADED

These rotate the head in one direction and then in the other.

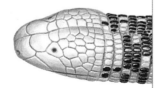

ROUND-HEADED

These push forward into the soil, and turn the head in any direction.

SHOVEL-HEADED

The shovel-heads push forward and then push the head up.

All about Snakes

There are almost 2,400 species of snakes. They range in size from the length of your arm to that of a small car. Snakes have many different colors, patterns, and ways of killing prey. They eat everything from ants, eggs, snails, and slugs to animals as big as caimans and goats. Some snakes kill by using venom, injected through their sharp fangs; others wrap themselves so tightly around their prey that the animal cannot breathe.

Shaped for Success

Snakes have different body shapes to suit their different environments. A ground-dwelling snake has an almost circular body. It has strong muscles to grip slippery surfaces such as sand and soil, or rough surfaces such as rocks. A tree snake's body is round at the top and flattened at the bottom and sides. This makes it easier to grip small crevices and notches on tree trunks and branches. A sea snake has a flattened body. This gives it a larger surface area with which to push against the water.

SEA SNAKE
The flattened body of a sea snake makes it a good swimmer.

DID YOU KNOW?

Vine snakes are so called because they are long and thin, and look like vines.

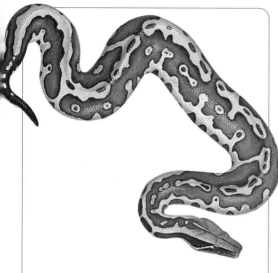

GROUND SNAKE
Ground dwellers have a body shape that is circular in cross-section—good for moving over most land surfaces.

TREE SNAKE
A tree snake glides through branches, thanks to a body that is shaped in cross-section almost like a loaf of bread.

The Long View

A snake is really just a long tube, which allows the animal to enter narrow crevices for food and shelter. But this tube varies greatly in size and shape from one snake group to another. The smallest snake is the 8 inch (20 cm) long thread snake; the largest is the giant anaconda, which can reach 36 feet (11 m) and weigh 440 pounds (200 kg). Snake bodies range from being shaped like a pencil to being shaped like a barrel.

RECORD HOLDER
The longest and heaviest of snakes, the anaconda of South America feeds on turtles, caimans, birds, fish, and mammals such as deer.

BODY SHAPES
Snakes have three general body shapes: small and slender (blind snake), short and thick-bodied (viper), and shaped like a cylinder (python).

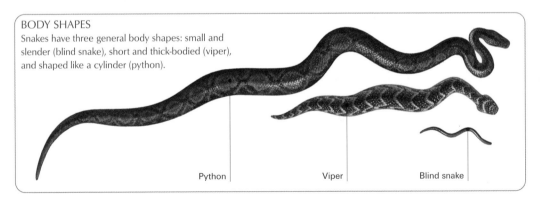

Python | Viper | Blind snake

Snake Heads

Snake heads give us clues about how and where snakes live.
For example, a tree snake has a slender head just wider than its
body, making it easier to move swiftly through vegetation. Most
pythons, however, live on the ground and hunt large animals.
Their heads are large enough to hold many teeth, which they
use to hold on to struggling prey. Most snakes can open their
jaws much wider than other reptiles.

DID YOU KNOW?

**The eastern hognose snake
uses its broad snout to dig
prey out of burrows.**

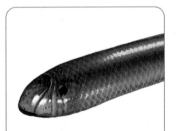

BURROWING SNAKE
A burrowing snake pushes through
the soil with a solid, blunt head.

TREE SNAKE
A tree snake has a slender head to
help it slip between twigs.

PYTHON
A python has a large head with powerful jaw muscles, which it uses to hold prey while it coils around the animal and squeezes it to death.

HORNED VIPER
Vipers have short, wide heads. The upper jaw is very short, with just a single large fang on either side. The wide head makes swallowing large prey easier.

Scales and Eyes

Snake skin is made up of scales. Freshwater snakes have keeled scales, which balance side-to-side movement. Snakes that burrow have smooth scales, as these make it easier to push through soil. Sea snakes have "granular" scales with a rough surface, which help them to grip fish. Eyes, too, tell us about a snake's habits. Burrowing snakes have small eyes; snakes with "cat's eye" pupils are active at night; those with large, round eyes are active in the day.

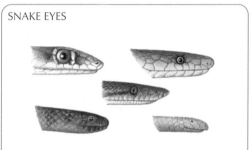

SNAKE EYES

Snake eyes vary from large round ones (daylight predators) to tiny (burrowing snakes that rarely see light).

A USEFUL SCALE
Most snakes have scales with a smooth, flat surface (far left). Some snakes have a ridge, called a keel, along the center of each scale (center). File snakes have rough, granular scales (left).

BIG EYES

Snakes active in the day need large eyes and good sight for hunting.

SMALL EYES

Night-hunters do not rely on sight to find prey and have small eyes.

EYES AT NIGHT

A snake's eyes are covered by a special clear eyelid that protects the eyes from damage. Nocturnal species often have vertical pupils, like the eyes of cats.

Shedding Skin

Snakes, like all reptiles, have a skin with an outer layer of thickened scales. As a snake grows, it sheds the dead outer layer of its scaly skin and reveals a new skin underneath. This may happen several times a year, depending on how fast the snake is growing. The old layer is not shed until a new one has completely formed underneath it. To loosen its skin, a snake rubs its nose against a hard surface and then wriggles free.

TAKE IT ALL OFF
A snake sheds its skin beginning with the head. As well as the skin of the body and head, the transparent, protective eye caps come off too.

DID YOU KNOW?
Each time a rattlesnake sheds its skin, its rattle gains a new segment.

PEELING AWAY
The old skin peels away in one piece, turning inside out as it comes off.

Snakes on the Move

Snakes have four ways to push their bodies along. A snake moves fast by pushing the side curves of its body against the surface it is traveling on (lateral undulation). In a narrow space, it presses its front coils against the sides of the space, then draws up the rest of the body (concertina movement). Heavy snakes crawl in a straight line by pushing back with sections of their belly while bringing other sections forward (rectilinear movement). Sidewinding is a way of moving on slippery surfaces, such as sand dunes.

FLYING SNAKE

The flying tree snake can glide from one tree to another.

LATERAL UNDULATION

Snakes move quickly by pushing against the ground.

CONCERTINA MOVEMENT

If they are in confined spaces, snakes move in a series of curves.

RECTILINEAR MOVEMENT

Some heavy-bodied snakes crawl in a straight line.

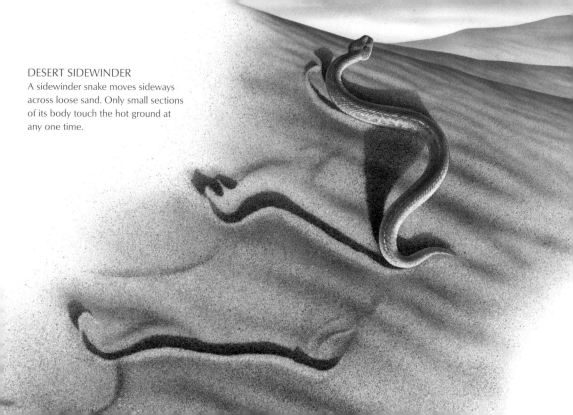

DESERT SIDEWINDER
A sidewinder snake moves sideways across loose sand. Only small sections of its body touch the hot ground at any one time.

The Inside Story

As snakes evolved from lizards, they became long and slender, and lost their limbs. Some internal organs, such as the liver and lungs, also became long and thin. Others, such as the kidneys and reproductive organs, were rearranged one behind the other in the body. In many snakes, the left lung disappeared.

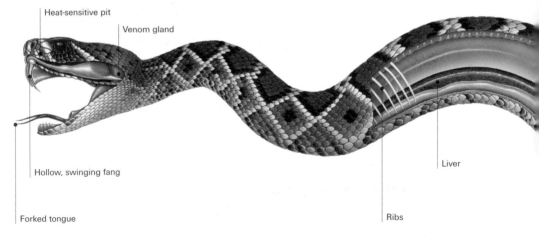

Heat-sensitive pit

Venom gland

Hollow, swinging fang

Forked tongue

Liver

Ribs

INSIDE A SNAKE

A snake, such as this rattlesnake, is like a stretched-out
cylinder. The internal organs are long and slender.

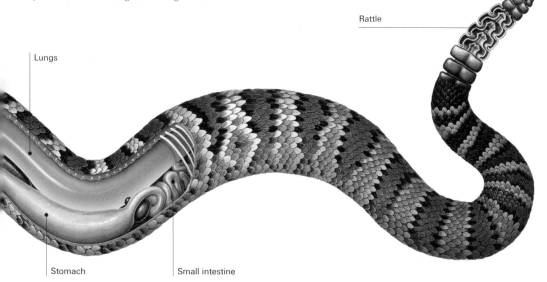

Rattle

Lungs

Stomach

Small intestine

Finding a Meal

All snakes eat animals. Some ambush, stalk, or pursue their prey. Others eat "easy" prey, such as the eggs of birds and reptiles. Many snakes, such as pythons, kill their prey by squeezing it. More than half of all snakes kill with venom, a poison injected through their fangs. Some snakes have small pits on their face that can detect heat from prey.

ON THE ATTACK
A rattlesnake's heat-sensing organs detect prey. Its fangs normally lie flat against the roof of its mouth and swing forward to inject venom.

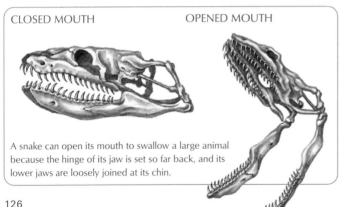

CLOSED MOUTH   OPENED MOUTH

A snake can open its mouth to swallow a large animal because the hinge of its jaw is set so far back, and its lower jaws are loosely joined at its chin.

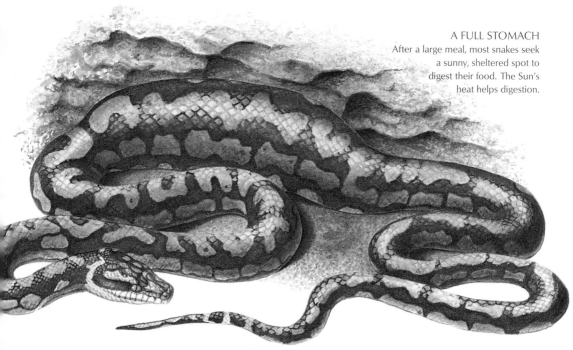

A FULL STOMACH
After a large meal, most snakes seek a sunny, sheltered spot to digest their food. The Sun's heat helps digestion.

Big Eater

Pythons are among the snakes that kill their prey by squeezing it. A python seizes its prey and wraps a series of coils around it. Whenever the prey breathes out, the python squeezes a little tighter. Eventually, the animal suffocates. A big python can swallow surprisingly large prey. It slowly "walks" its jaws forward to engulf an animal as large as a wild pig.

Sudden Death

Some snakes, such as rattlesnakes, bite and kill their prey with a poison called venom. The venom is produced in mouth glands and comes out through the snake's fangs. The prey dies within minutes, sometimes even seconds.

Types of Fangs

Venomous snakes have different kinds of fangs. Some are firmly attached to the jaw while others are hinged; some are grooved while others are hollow; some are in front of the mouth and others are at the rear. Snakes with hollow fangs inject venom into their prey, while snakes with grooved fangs let the venom ooze into the victim.

COTTONMOUTH
This venomous cottonmouth pit viper has hinged front fangs.

REAR FANGS

Venom duct

Fangs are fixed in the rear of the mouth; fangs have grooves.

FIXED FRONT FANGS

Venom duct

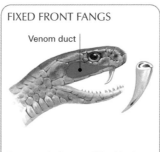

Fangs are hollow and fixed in the front of the mouth.

SWINGING FRONT FANGS

Venom duct

Fangs are hollow and swing forward to the front of the mouth.

Mother Care

In species that lay eggs, the female snake lays her eggs in a safe, warm, and slightly moist place, such as a beneath a rock. In most species, she covers the eggs and leaves them. Some snakes give birth to fully developed young. But in all cases, young snakes fend for themselves.

MOTHER'S WATCHING
Some pythons coil around their eggs to keep them warm and protect them from predators. Although she cares for the eggs, the mother leaves them when they have hatched.

ON THEIR OWN
Female snakes do not look after their young once the eggs have hatched. These young snakes will soon be on their own.

Growing Up Green

Green pythons from the rain forests of New Guinea and northern Australia do not start out green. When they hatch, they are bright yellow or brick brown in color. They become the green color of adults after one to three years.

Defense Tactics

Snakes have many enemies. They are killed and eaten by fish, lizards, other snakes, birds of prey, and mammals. They have a number of ways to defend themselves. Some camouflage or bury themselves to hide from danger. Other snakes surprise their enemies by making themselves look bigger, hissing, or lashing out with their bodies. Still others keep perfectly still, as many predators depend on movement to find their prey. There are also snakes that rely on speed for escape, moving quickly into a burrow or up a tree.

RATTLESNAKE KILLER

A king snake is not harmed by rattlesnake venom.

PLAYING DEAD

The hog-nosed snake plays dead to confuse attackers.

A FRIGHTENING SIGHT
The vine snake opens wide its brightly colored mouth to startle predators.

RATTLING DEFENSE
When disturbed, a rattlesnake will vibrate its tail to make a loud rattling sound, diverting attention to the tail and away from the striking head.

Warning Colors

Some snakes rely on bright colors to let predators know they are venomous. Red and orange, in various combinations, are the most common colors that signal danger to a predator. A few non-venomous snakes even mimic these colors.

KEEP AWAY?
Although most eyelash pit vipers of Central and South America are camouflaged in green and brown, some are this bright orange color. Perhaps it warns possible predators to beware.

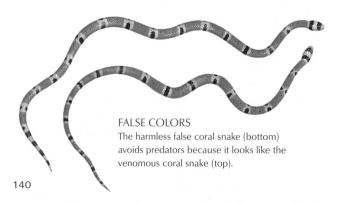

FALSE COLORS
The harmless false coral snake (bottom) avoids predators because it looks like the venomous coral snake (top).

Tuataras

The tuatara has changed little in 240 million years. It is often referred to as a "living fossil." Found only on small islands off the coast of New Zealand, tuataras are the oldest living relatives of today's snakes and lizards. The gray, olive, or reddish tuatara is not a lizard at all. The two species of tuataras are the only living members of a group of small- to medium-sized reptiles called Rhynchocephalia, or "beak-heads." Rhynchocephalians lived in most parts of the world while the dinosaurs were alive. But by 60 million years ago, they were extinct everywhere except New Zealand, which had become isolated from other landmasses.

Slowly Disappearing?

Tuataras were once found throughout the two main islands of New Zealand. Apart from birds, tuataras faced no large predators until the arrival of humans a few thousand years ago. The settlers brought with them rats and dogs, and these animals began to eat tuatara eggs and hatchlings. Today, tuataras can be found only on islands without rats.

DID YOU KNOW?

Tuataras keep growing for 35 years, and may live for more than 100 years.

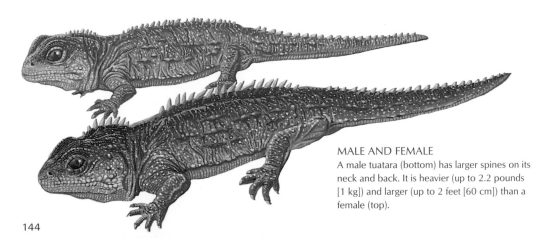

MALE AND FEMALE
A male tuatara (bottom) has larger spines on its neck and back. It is heavier (up to 2.2 pounds [1 kg]) and larger (up to 2 feet [60 cm]) than a female (top).

NIGHT BEAT
Tuataras hunt insects and other prey at night. They spend the day sleeping in their burrows or basking in the sunshine at their burrow entrances.

Where Do Reptiles Live?

Reptiles occur across most of the world's landmasses and in many oceans and seas. They are sensitive to temperature, and the number of species decreases toward the polar regions, until eventually they drop out altogether. Most species are found in tropical and subtropical areas.

TURTLES
Turtles are found on all continents except Antarctica, and in all oceans: 241 species of turtles have adapted to freshwater rivers, lakes, and ponds; 45 tortoises live on land; seven species live in the oceans.

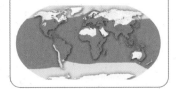

CROCODILIANS
Crocodilians are found in all tropical, subtropical, and temperate zones: gharials in South Asia; crocodiles in Africa, South Asia, Australia, and Central and South America; and alligators in China and the Americas.

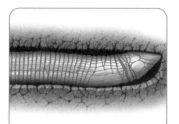

AMPHISBAENIANS

Amphisbaenians are found in tropical and subtropical regions of southern North America, South America to Patagonia, West Indies, Africa, Spain, Portugal, Arabia, and western Asia.

TUATARA

The two species of tuataras live on New Zealand islands. About 400 *Sphenodon guntheri* live on North Brother Island. More than 60,000 *S. punctatus* live on about 30 islands off the North Island.

LIZARDS

Lizards are found across a vast area of the world, from New Zealand to Norway, and from southern Canada to Tierra del Fuego. They also live on many of the islands in the world's oceans.

147

Reptiles around the World

The map shows the vegetation zones of the world. Which animals live in a particular area depends on the vegetation of that area. Reptiles mostly live in deserts, tropical forests, and tropical grasslands. They are not found as often in mountainous regions, on tundra, and in icy regions such as the Arctic.

Tropical forest
Seasonal tropical forest
Desert
Tropical grassland and savanna
Mediterranean forest and scrub
Midlatitude grassland
Midlatitude forest
Boreal forest
Tundra
Ice sheet
Mountain vegetation

TROPICAL LIZARD
The frilled lizard is found in tropical Australia's dry woodlands, where it feeds mainly on large insects.

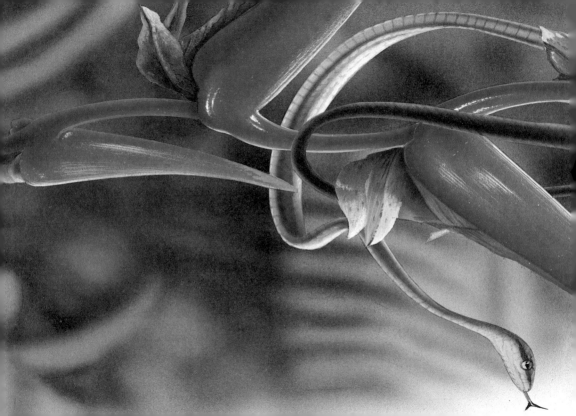

GLOSSARY
AND INDEX

Glossary

adaptation A change that occurs in an animal's behavior or body form to allow it to survive and breed in new conditions.

amphibian A vertebrate that can live on land and in water. Amphibians (frogs and toads, salamanders and newts, and caecilians) are similar to reptiles, but they have moist skin and they lay their eggs in water.

aquatic Living in water all or most of the time.

arboreal Living in trees all or most of the time.

arthropod An animal with jointed legs and a hard external skeleton. Insects, spiders, crustaceans, centipedes, and millipedes are all arthropods.

bask To hold the body in a position directly exposed to the sun's rays.

camouflage The colors and patterns of an animal that enable it to blend in with the background.

carapace The upper part of a chelonian's shell.

carnivore An animal that eats only meat.

chelonian A turtle or tortoise. A member of the order Chelonia.

cocoon In amphibians, a case made of mud, mucus, or similar material, in which the animal rests.

courtship The behavior of animals that ultimately results in mating.

crest In lizards, a line of large, scaly spines on the neck and back.

crocodilian A crocodile, alligator, caiman, or gharial. A member of the order Crocodilia.

crustacean A mostly aquatic animal, such as a lobster, crab, or prawn, that has a hard external skeleton.

dewlap In a lizard, a flap of skin on the throat.

display Behavior used by an animal to communicate with its own species, or with other animals. Displays, which include postures, actions, or showing brightly colored parts of the body, may signal threat, defense, or readiness to mate.

ectothermic Unable to keep the body at a stable, warm temperature by internal means. Reptiles and amphibians are ectothermic but maintain a high body temperature by behavior, for example by basking in the sun.

embryo An unborn animal in the earliest stages of development.

endangered In danger of becoming extinct.

endothermic Able to regulate body temperature by internal means, regardless of the outside temperature. Birds and mammals are endothermic.

environment All the natural features of Earth, such as landforms and climate, that affect living things.

evolution The gradual change in plants and animals, over many generations, in response to their environment.

extinct Of a species, no longer in existence.

frill A collar around a lizard's neck.

gastroliths Stones swallowed by animals such as crocodilians, that stay in the stomach and help crush food.

gill An organ that absorbs oxygen from water.

habitat The place where an animal naturally lives. Many different kinds of animals live in the same environment, but each kind lives in a different habitat within that environment.

hatchling A young animal, such as a bird or reptile, that has recently hatched from its egg.

herbivore An animal that eats only plant material, such as leaves.

invertebrate An animal that does not have a backbone. Many invertebrates are soft-bodied animals, but most, such as insects, have a hard external skeleton.

larva (plural larvae) A young animal that looks completely different from its parents. In amphibians, the larval stage is the stage before metamorphosis that breathes with gills rather than lungs (for example, tadpoles).

metamorphosis A way of development in which an animal's body changes shape over a short period of time. Amphibians undergo metamorphosis as they grow to maturity.

mimicry A strategy by which an animal copies or imitates another animal, either to hunt or to avoid being hunted.

neoteny The retention by an animal of some immature or larval characteristics into adulthood.

plastron The lower part of a chelonian's shell.

predator An animal that hunts or preys on other animals for its food.

prey An animal that is hunted by predators.

reptile An ectothermic vertebrate with dry, scaly skin. Tortoises, turtles, snakes, lizards, and crocodilians are reptiles.

scales In reptiles, thickened areas of skin that vary in size.

scutes In chelonians, the horny plates that cover the bony shell.

species A group of animals with very similar features that are able to breed together and produce fertile young.

tadpole The larva of a frog or toad. Tadpoles live in water and take in oxygen through gills.

temperate Describes a region or environment that has a warm (but not very hot) summer and a cool (but not very cold) winter.

territory An area of land inhabited by an animal and defended by it.

toxin Poisonous substance produced by a plant or animal.

tropical Describes a region or environment near the Equator that is warm to hot all year round.

venom Poison injected by animals into a predator or prey through fangs, spines, or similar structures.

venomous Describes an animal that delivers a venom.

vertebrate An animal with a backbone—an internal skeleton of cartilage or bone. Fish, reptiles, birds, amphibians, and mammals are all vertebrates.

Index

Acknowledgments

PHOTOGRAPHIC CREDITS

Key t=top; l=left; r=right; tl=top left; tcl=top center left; tc=top center; tcr=top center right; tr=top right; cl=center left; c=center; cr=center right; b=bottom; bl=bottom left; bcl=bottom center left; bc=bottom center; bcr=bottom center right; br=bottom right

COR = Corel Corp. DV = Digital Vision; iS = istockphoto.com; PD = Photodisc; PE = PhotoEssentials; PL = photolibrary.com

27c COR **31**l iS **32**l, r COR **33**c COR **34**r COR **37**c PD **40**l COR **58**b iS **63**br COR **65**c COR **67**c COR **75**c COR **84**br iS **85**c PD **86**br COR **88**l, r COR **91**c DV **99**c PE **102**bl PL **105**c COR **109**t PL **115**c COR **119**l COR **120**br iS **121**c PL **133**c COR **139**c COR **141**c COR

ILLUSTRATION CREDITS

Alistar Barnard, Anne Bowman, Barbara Rodanska, Christer Eriksson, Colin Newman/Bernard Thornton Artists UK, David Kirshner, Fiammetta Dogi, Frank Knight, James McKinnon, John Francis/Bernard Thornton Artists UK, Jon Gittoes, Ken Oliver/The Art Agency, Kevin Stead, Map Illustrations, MagicGroup s.r.o (Czech Republic)—www.magicgroup.cz, Peter Schouten, Rob Mancini, Robert Hynes, Rod Westblade, Roger Swainston, Simone End, Tony Pyrzakowski, Trevor Ruth

INDEX

Ken DellaPenta

CONSULTANT

Dr Mark Hutchinson is the Researcher in Herpetology at the South Australian Museum, where he has worked since 1990. His research has included studies of reptile and amphibian biology and evolution, the classification and evolution of Australian lizards, and the distribution and conservation of reptiles in Australia.